Anna's poetry addresses and remedy: God's Spirit working through Jesus Christ. It's for every hurting soul who desires to gain inspiration and wisdom from a caring soul quite familiar with ongoing pain, yet Anna has come through this singing, surrendering, and serving God and others. The overarching revelation is this: no seasoned believer evades suffering nor has to remain there as the defeated sufferer. In fact, our night's weeping helps in defining us for God and is often discovered in the dark silence of suffering when we finally come to realize that He is always there with us as the only true way out of our seemingly endless stream of pain and problems. The Silent Wind eventually blows away the clouds, the locust, and that foul stench of death from our lives so that the blueness and warmth of God's sky and sea may be fully realized and appreciated.

Claudia Cobian De Soto, mother, pastor's wife and
Co-owner of Cobian Corp., San Marcos, CA
Claudia De Soto
Cobian USA

Silent Wind's biblical poetry blows open reality's door much better than straight prose. It's an imaginary expanse of crystal blue ocean with real dolphins and otters playing within it, declaring that the Spirit's silent wind guides your sail across the perilous seas of post-modernity and places your feet onto loving heaven's peaceful shore. Every page makes you keenly aware of this gracious, sovereign presence, the Silent Wind of God's providential hands guiding your life's voyage to eternity's other side.

Bruce De Soto, Pastor-Theologian of
The Church on the Hill, Vista, Ca
tel: (760) 734-1915 x 306
fax: (760) 734-1917
www.cobianusa.com

Anna's poetry takes me back to great moments in my past including my childhood. God had given her a magnificent and special gift which she uses with love and grace when she reads before our church. She speaks for those who can't. I admire her words of faith. She has courage to let others see the soft and delicate part of herself. Her poetry I have related to my own life, and has opened my eyes to not fear in using my own gifts God has given to me.

John A. Yarbrough
Church on the Hill-member

THE SILENT WIND

To sweet Charlotte!

Love,
Anna

Bless you always!

THE *Silent Wind*

AC LEVENSON

TATE PUBLISHING
AND ENTERPRISES, LLC

Published by Tate Publishing & Enterprises, LLC
127 E. Trade Center Terrace | Mustang, Oklahoma 73064 USA
1.888.361.9473 | www.tatepublishing.com

Tate Publishing is committed to excellence in the publishing industry. The company reflects the philosophy established by the founders, based on Psalm 68:11,
"The Lord gave the word and great was the company of those who published it."

Book design copyright © 2015 by Tate Publishing, LLC. All rights reserved.
Cover design by Charito Sim
Interior design by Jomar Ouano

Published in the United States of America

ISBN: 978-1-63449-991-0
Poetry / Subjects & Themes / Inspirational & Religious
15.07.02

I dedicate this book to our Lord who blesses me mightily, protects me, and loves me like I have never known.

I also dedicate this book to my husband, Brian who I love with all my heart.

To my children who I am very proud of and love very deeply— Lauren, John, and Shanna.

To my mom, Maryjane, who believed in me, loved me, encouraged me, loved my father, and took care of him until he passed away. (A love we all should know.)

Praise God for giving me the words through prayer to help others that are hurting or struggling.

Acknowledgments

I would like to express my deepest
appreciation to my pastor,
Pastor Bruce De Soto

He believed in me when I stopped believing in myself from a tragedy that occurred in my life. Pastor De Soto gave me counsel, interventions in my life, advice, and his consistent teachings about our Lord and Savior. His sermons have touched my life, my husband, and many people through-out the city. Pastor De Soto leads two churches: the Church on the Hill in San Diego (Vista) and the Vine House Christian Church in San Clemente; both churches are located in California. Pastor De Soto is an ordained Calvary Chapel pastor who has been ministering North County, San Diego, for the last twenty-six years. The Lord has blessed him with the gift of teaching that helps the heart to grow in God. I would also like to acknowledge the first lady of the church, his wife, Claudia De Soto, who gives her all to everyone around her including all the children of our church. I would like to add a special thank you for Pastor Chuck Smith of Calvary Chapel Costa Mesa, my pastor of many years throughout my life, who taught so much about the Lord and who touched my heart with his teachings.

> And I will give you pastors according
> to my heart, which shall feed you with
> knowledge and understanding.
>
> —Jeremiah 3:15

To the glory of God

True greatness is not measured by the headlines a person commands or the wealth he or she accumulates, The inner character of a person—the undergirding moral and spiritual values and commitments—is the true measure of lasting greatness.

—Billy Graham

CONTENTS

PART VII SHARING THE LIGHT

PART VIII HAND IN HAND

INTRODUCTION

This book will take you through a poetic journey into the heart of relationships. These poems convey messages from people's lives and through prayer that correlates with Bible scripture that is intended for anyone wanting or needing peace and hope in their life. It involves a relationship with God and with fellow man. Life is a journey fought with many turns and challenges when there are times of great vantage points and, in other times, it may be just the trudge of moving onward, and, of course, there are those darker moments when joy and love seem to disappear.

These poems are intended to serve as signposts along the way of life. They are used to bring a new perspective to your heart on God and how He gives us strength, direction, love, and joy. These poems are used by pastors, churches, ministry professionals, families, Bible study groups, self-help groups, support classes, and anyone needing strength to rise above and understand there is a God who loves us. This collection of poems reflects the journey forward toward home to be with our Lord.

Though I walk in the mist of trouble,
You will revive me: and you will stretch
out your hand against the wrath of my
enemies, and your right hand shall save
me.

—Psalms 138:7

Part I

Passions

A Hurricane Named Desire

What a beautiful day, so warm and so bright,
the winds are so still, and you, my Lord, right in
my sight.
I feel your grace as you pour down upon me
the sweetest and greatest of love that can ever be.

Something is coming, the clouds start to appear,
the roar of the thunder as lightening brings fear.
The howl of the day that was clear and so warm
comes in unexpected as I run for the door.

The twirl and whirl of the wind churning on through
come now with the thunder and lightning in view.
The sky turned to black and the day turns to dark.
I will ride out this force with the grace of your
mark.

That will carry me in all the right ways
to make a difference when life becomes a haze.
To live for your love and your path in my life,
no matter what storm tries to steal and make strife.

When the day comes from the clear of the storm,
you may stand in a place where your heart
becomes warm.
For you came to know how to steer the right way,
no matter the hardships of things taken away.

We have to pull through during the hardest times.
It is then that we know we can surely rise.
For the shine of the day even in the darkest hour,
becomes all brand new in God's love and power

I never knew this walk I would take.
I thought maybe my path was a mistake.
But no! it was real and the way it should be, for
I rose to the mark so my Lord would see.

I learned the good fight down a very hard road.
To withstand what did come in the heart of
the storm.
So we all should rise and come to know,
we can take what has come that will help us
to grow.

The plan has been laid, so follow Him would
be best.
This will carry the love deep into your chest.
You will rise to the top and in his grace you
will glow.
You've broken free from the storm being led
down a new road.

Be strong and courageous. Do not fear
or be in dread of them, for it is the Lord
your God who goes with you. He will
not leave you or forsake you.

—Deuteronomy 31:6

When the righteous cry for help, the
Lord hears and delivers them out of all
their troubles. The Lord is near to the
brokenhearted and saves the crushed
in spirit. Many are the afflictions of
the righteous, but the Lord delivers
him out of them all. He keeps all his
bones; not one of them is broken.

—Psalms 34:17

The Lord sits enthroned over the flood;
He sits enthroned as king forever. May
the Lord give strength to His people!b
May the Lord bless His people with
peace!

—Psalms 29:10–11

Craving Hope

The light does turn red at times in our lives,
that can knock the breath out of our hearts.
When changes come to capture us,
that can tear our hearts apart.

Our reaction does not always seem to glow,
when we cannot and do not understand.
But hold onto the truth and pray with all
you have,
knowing the hope will soon take full command.

Love and hope are what we really seek in all the
things we do.
With the simple hope that day will come,
when this craving becomes brand-new.

It could be sickness, disease, or loss that might
come knocking through.
Perhaps we want to just have the hope that
comes into clear view.
Wherefore gird up the loins of your mind and
be sober too,
for the revelation of our Lord brings hope, love,
and grace to you.

Stay on the simple path of finding joys that fill
your heart.
Hope will come; just do not give up when the
changes come to mark.
Your lives in ways that can steal your breath
when you lose your way.
It is our faith we choose to keep in our hearts
each and every day.

Why am I discouraged? Why is my
heart so sad? I will put my hope in God!
I will praise him again-my Savior and
my God!

—Psalms 42:11

THE SECRET GARDEN

How is it when life can be hard but some seem to find the green?
the leaves all falling to the ground from things that are not seen.
But then the door just opens wide to take us to the place,
where flowers bloom bright that brings our hearts sweet grace.

How do we even understand when someone that we touch,
goes through a garden of rocks and stones that hurts us very much?
How do we pull into the place of beauty and of rest?
To a garden made inside our hearts where beauty makes us our best.

I see it now all in my mind as I hold onto my loved one's hand.
I feel the love flow through me as if he still understands.

I wander off into the place I know will bring
me joy,
a place of sweet smell and beauty that even now
I can employ.

So when I'm told how can you smile while
standing in the rough.
I say we can get through to a secret garden that's
a must.
To get there, simply open the door and smell
sweet flowers and pine.
You will know you're in the special place, a peace
you will find.

A secret garden is the place we hold the very best.
To make a hardship very strong and rise above
the rest,
to always feel and always know we can escape
the pain,
to unleash your soul and hold to faith while
stopping ongoing pain.

So onward as our lives go forth to make a
difference here,
To knowing we can open the door to a garden
that releases fear,

that, in our minds, our hearts, and souls, we can
take a hardship down,
to arrive into the place where the secret garden
is truly found.

> Come and see what our God has done,
> what awesome miracles he performs for
> people
>
> —Psalm 66:5

THE BRAZEN SUN

I see the path that I must walk; it's become so
clear to me.
Knowing now this path that's laid, I am now
set free.
The path is long with winding ways taking me
through the fields.
Back again, it comes around to be the warmth
that I can feel.

I may not know what's wrong but along the path
I see,
the light and grace of our Lord that matter most
to me.
I have gotten lost along the way but came
back around,
all to know the reasons were to see that I was
found.

Accept the changes along the way no matter
what does come.
To believe that all the love God gave when he
gave to us his Son.

 AC LEVENSON

Is to keep the journey close to Him who gives
to us His all,
that along the path in the brazen sun, your love
becomes His song.

The bold and brazen sun does rise and gives us
warmth when cold.
Knowing that in your life, you see the beauty
rise and unfold.
Our Lord made everything so beautiful to see,
no matter what you're going through, He brings
the sweet relief.

I sit along the ocean shore as the sun rises to
the east.
The brazen sun is bright with warmth as God
made it to be.
Your heart will fill the warmth each step you
make to eternity.
Hold the course along the way as God's love
shapes what will be.

For by grace you are saved through faith;
and that not of yourselves: it is a gift
from God.

—Ephesians 2:8

THE CHAMPION

The champion walks with confidence in our Lord,
the quiet, soft-spoken ways that all can adore.
When the rain does pour, the strength comes strong,
for the love of our Lord is the music of his song.

We all can fall from hurt and pain.
The Lord will keep us and help to refrain.
From all that comes to blow us down,
the mighty champion whose strong faith is sound

The champion turns to our Lord in prayer,
where he strives for the love and life with less error.
But even in the times of battle,
he girds up his strength and sits high on the saddle.

Oh! How the mighty champion will win.
To grow in the strength of the lessons that spin.
To bring in the grace that comes to the heart.
When he know God is there and will never part.

Waking again to the sound of the strife,
now rising quickly to the battles of life.
The champion will pray to help get him through.
For the path that he chooses will arise in clear view.

The peace and the love shines bright all around.
For the champion's ways are on hallowed ground.
The life we can change and become new,
Is the joy in our hearts from God's perfect queue.

Who is that champion we can choose to be?
With the strength from God's grace, he can now finally see.
He recognizes all the wrongs and makes it right, the champion who changes and finds a completely new life.

> For the Lord God is a sun and shield;
> the Lord will give grace and glory: no
> good thing will He withhold from them
> that walk uprightly.
>
> —Psalms 84:11

The Lord Reigns on High

Blessed are those who wash their robes to enter through the gates,
into the kingdom of our Lord where all His love is made.
To bring us up and lay to rest the place we thought and longed.
To the kingdom our Lord reigns where pain and suffering are gone.

How beautiful on the mountain tops from those who bring the news,
that peace and salvation reigns singing a song of being renewed.
The end of the earth will see the salvation of our God,
and turning to the only place when heaven is only sought.

The place where man may rise free from his sentence,
to fall down unto your knees in deep repentance.

The rain and snow come down from the mountains to the sea.
Our Lord opened up the flood gates so that we can be set free.

The spirit of the Lord God can come into your life.
He will lift you up into his arms and take you from the strife.
His faithful mercies show the forgiveness and the love.
He has risen up a horn of salvation to bring us up above.

Shout for joy, do not cry, lift your eyes from the earth.
The Lord reigns into our lives and has formed a new birth.
Take the only path that will glorify His name.
Change your life forever for Our Lord reigns.

The sun, the moon, the stars to the hills and the plains.
Are not these, O' Soul the vision of Him who reigns.
God is the law, say the wise, let us rejoice!

For if He thunders by the law, by the law is yet
His voice.

Dreams are true while they last, do we not live
in dreams?
God is the vision and so it might not be what
it seems.
Earth these solid stars, this weight of body
and limb.
The signs and symbols of our Lord is the way
to Him.

Grace be with all of them that love our
Lord Jesus Christ in sincerity.

—Ephesians 6:24

THE PROMISE MADE

The time has passed from days of lore.
To uphold the ways as a servant's chore.
To rise again to uplift in a place,
to find that path in His heavenly grace.

To unwind the past will make you strong,
to feel the grace which you have longed.
You will finally come to feel so safe,
for the promise made has given way.

Here I sit again in wonder,
coming from the war of thunder.
To realize we can serve and be the best.
Walking through fire where there is no rest.

His promise we can hold deep in our hearts,
standing strong as a warrior that will never impart.
The reason will make since of what we do
not understand.
Finding all along it was all in our Lord's command.

To take us through what we must to change,
to rise to the mark where our Lord's love is made.

To carry spiritual weapons that will destroy evil
that employs.
That brings in the changes that we can finally
enjoy.

The blood, sweat, and tears we come all the
way through,
will only help you coming into God's clear view.
He knows our hearts, and he knows our ways,
so the path that is made for you will never sway.

Our Lord tells us whatever things we ask when
we pray,
we will receive them, and they will come our way.
Just hold the course and do not sway dig in
your heels,
the time will come when all your prayers are
revealed.

> Therefore I say to you, whatever things
> you ask when you pray, believe and you
> receive them and you will have them.
>
> —Mark 11:24

The Resurrection

Jesus came to earth to show us how to live,
how to put others first, how to love, and how
to give.
Then He took our punishment all onto himself.
He did this for all of us to show our way to
true health.

He died and rose again so we would learn
the way.
He chose to pay our price for sin to know not
to stray.
Our Lord did this out of love so we could learn
to know,
that choosing right and living for Him will help
us all to grow.

Jesus made it possible for all who would believe.
We can all experience eternal life with our eyes
open to see.
Today is a day for meaningful worship to begin.
This is what we carry each day to take away
our sins.

Our Lord changed everything through His
physical resurrection.
Through God's grace, we've been enabled
to partake,
in the life with Christ as new creations.

Christ's resurrection disarmed and triumphed
over the enemy of our souls.
We are now able to take the path he designed
for us to know,
we all understand what employs that the cross
did not destroy.
His resurrection on Easter morn just fills our
hearts with joy.

We do not merely need for our minds to be
made right for our soul.
We need everything broken, everything indi-
vidual, every nation,
every injustice, all of creation to be made whole.

Jesus endured a kind of pain and suffering we
cannot begin to fathom.
No depiction of what he endured can truly do
justice on what happened.

   AC LEVENSON

Even the disciples were bewildered and slow to
recognize their friend.
Knowing the resurrection was just the beginning
and not the end.

Jesus was raised to life; we are now able to
experience a new life with Him.
The result is that we are free to no longer be
mastered by sin.
So let us live our lives for Jesus and think of Him
in all we do.
Thank you, Savior; thank you, Lord,
Help us love each other just like you.

> Jesus Himself personifies life and the
> power to bring what is dead back to
> life; we experience this reality through
> relationship with Him.
>
> —John 11:25–26

THE SILENT WIND

It does not matter what time it is,
in the morning, day, or night.
The loss of you breaks right on through.
I feel the breeze in my chair by the light.

I always think and remember back,
on all my life here with you,
the little things, the big ones too,
then the wind breaks right on through.

I have to hold on tight some days,
to understand the loss of you.
I know the reason now was something that
you knew.
Then the breeze from the window comes through.

I wake each day with an empty feel,
so I go outside for awhile.
I stand on the lawn and look at the sky,
when the breeze hits my face and I smile.

You're always there.
You're with me still,
although I want to feel your touch.
No matter where I am to be,
your love from the wind lifts me up.

> You will restore me even to greater
> honor and comfort me once again.

> —Psalms 71:21

THE WAR'S BEEN WON

The battle grounds of life itself comes in so mighty strong.
The fury of the rage that comes scrapes and scares and numbs.
Do remember this war has come because the path was laid.
To turn our lives and lift it up to heaven's golden gate.

I stand in awe of grace that comes when I can push aside my pain.
To become humble within myself that clears the wound and stain.
Great is our Lord to be praised for what he gives our hearts.
The wars been won; He died for us so we can have a new start.

Mistakes I've made from choices past I could not see so clear.
I did know that our Lord would take away all my fears.

Through learning with wisdom and words our Lord will give,
bringing us to the battlefield to understand we must forgive.

The war's been won all for us who believe the words from God.
To stand at battle in the raging fire to be lifted up above.
On we go to march along the path that He did lay.
The war's been won to know the truth and pray for His wisdom and ways.

> But He gives us more grace.
> God opposes the proud,
> But gives grace unto the humble.

> —James 4:6

Change of Life

Did you ever think your life could change?
After waiting so long prayers unanswered and strained.
To try and make sense that will keep you alive.
To bring in the sweetness, of strong faith just in time.

To bring up the helm and steer to the east,
to see the bright star, when you felt defeat.
Your life goes asunder and wondering why,
as the wind of change comes in strong and alive.

The days, nights, and years pass on through.
Nothing seems to fit and desperate comes in view.
We stumble when our heart becomes restless,
churning to places when the past never erases.

The wind then comes in strong and blows to our heart.
We lift our prayers asking God, "Is this the new start?"

Will it leave and I start to slide back to that place, where the lonely just lingers and we feel the disgrace.

The magic in the moment we begin to withstand.
Our strength comes in furry to a magnificent plan.
One that we thought could never blow through.
To find the wind of change was the beginning of the new.

Hold onto the promise the Lord gave us to know.
To live in our faith as we learn and we grow.
To never give up for the change will come in,
your life may feel asunder as the wind of change begins.

> You have allowed me to suffer much
> hardship, but you will restore me to life
> again and lift me up to the depths of the
> earth
>
> —Psalms 71:20

Part II

We Are Not Alone

A Special Prayer

It is all so very clear to me,
the open and closed doors.
You bring me sweet release,
and I pray I just want more

I pray for your will and way,
as my life changes inside of me.
You make it known the hidden truth,
That brings me to my knees.

You have been my protection,
like I've never known.
Will this life be good to me,
or betray my comfort zone?

Will I know just where I stand,
amongst the thistles and thorns.
Finding my way, all when I pray,
when you close and open doors.

Forgive me, Lord, with all my heart,
you give me everything.
But most of all your protection,
takes away the pain and sting.

Do I stay here to the end?
Will the passion in my heart begin?
A hunger thirst of a brand new song,
to be loved with whom I am and where I belong.

But I realize deep in my soul,
I will know just where to go,
because the truth, wisdom stands me tall,
the teaching of doing right most of all!

Forgive me if I do anything wrong,
you have been so good to me all along.
Your protection, love, and loyalty,
that always brings me to my knees.

> May the words of my mouth and the
> meditation of my heart be pleasing
> to you, Oh Lord, my rock and my
> redeemer.
>
> —Psalms 19:14

Merciful Raindrops

Do I speak and act as though I am going to be judged by the law?
In any moments of temptation, does my weakness become the flaw?
Bind me about my neck; let not mercy and truth forsake thee,
write me upon the table of my heart that will surely set me free.

The merciful man does well for his own soul through the test,
but he that is cruel troubles his own flesh.
Oh, my Lord, all I know is I want to give you my best.
As the rain pours down upon the body of my chest.

I stand in the mist of the drops of rain falling down.
Like the mercy you give that shows your staff and crown.
To take hold of the life we fail to see.
As you come to us giving all your love and mercy.

You say, my Lord, put on a heart of compassion,
kindness, humility, gentleness, and patience;
bearing with one another, and forgiving each
other, whoever has a complaint against anyone;
just as you forgave us, so also should we.

It is your merciful rain that sets us free!
I will be glad and rejoice in your mercy.

For you have considered my trouble; you have
known my soul in adversities.
So again, I cry out on days just like these,
Oh please, my dear Lord, show me merciful
mercies.

We have come to know the truth of your hope.
That takes us much higher than any path we
can cope.
We try but will not make to be even the glimmer
of you.
You still hold us in your arms so your love shines
on through.

If we should fail as we seem to do.
We know that your love will always be true.

 AC LEVENSON

Determined in our hearts to make decisions that
are blessed,
to come through the storms when our faith will
give us rest.

Oh, merciful rains just pour right on down.
To flood my life that can make me frown.
I will show you my love and the way I should be.
Through my actions I live for your mercies to me.

> Speak and act as those who are going
> to be judged by the law that gives
> freedom, because judgment without
> mercy will be shown to anyone who has
> not been merciful. Mercy triumphs over
> judgment.
>
> —James 2:12–13

The Face of the Sea

I sit on edge of the blues and greens,
where the ocean and sun shines to the highest
gleam.
It reaches my soul and takes me away.
To the uncharted path of the cylinder lighting
my way.

Oh, I know when in moments like this.
Through the barriers, life brings the unwanted
shifts.
To the light of the moments when darkness
can fall,
that circles the brilliance of beauty that draws.

I take on the wings of the morning that swells,
to the utmost of glimmer that no longer fails.
I know He will lead me and hold my right hand.
The pain will release in the day on the sand.

Looking and seeking your love and grace.
Where I feel you this moment where no
glimmers erased.

Just the warmth of the beauty you bring to
my heart.
That takes me in moments to knowing my mark.

To rise up above knowing you're always there.
Finding the peace in your face as I stare
Into the beauty you give to my heart,
as the glimmer and brilliance of the sea are
your art.

Here in the moment I come to myself.
In knowing and growing what needs to be felt.
To give into all just to rest in your place.
The face of the sea where the pain can erase.

He has inscribed a circle on the face of
the waters at the boundary between light
and darkness.

—Job 26:10

The purpose in a man's heart is like deep
water, but a man of understanding will
draw it out.

—Proverbs 20:5

If I take the wings of the morning and
dwell in the uttermost parts of the sea,
even there your hand shall lead me, and
your right hand shall hold me.

—Psalms 139:9–10

 AC LEVENSON

THE GIRL WHO RIDES THE WAVES

I paddled out into the waves,
I tumbled all around.
I could not stand on my own two feet,
I was thrown into the dark ocean sound.

I lifted my head to take a breath,
But many times it turned so dark.
Being pulled down so long and hard,
I still fought and held my mark.

Nothing changed throughout this ride
perhaps a bump and merge of rage.
I never knew or understood,
the point that was being made.

All along the waves I rode,
became such harmony,
no matter when it hit me hard,
I learned to lift my head to breathe.

So beautiful it is to see,
the wonderful blues and greens.
Even during the harmful rides,
all I saw was the ocean gleams.

I reflect back,
when I rode those waves,
what I learned and what I know.
God saw the tragic hand
He protected me from the blows.

I know now the plan was clear,
The waves were meant to be.
The difficult places I rode into,
has set my life so free.

I rest now into a brand new wave,
one I know I can ride well.
The training and the discipline,
taught me how to glide into the swell.

So if I ride the stormy curves,
the waves that I did survive.
This will bring a peace in me,
because our Lord is along my side.

Be strong and courageous, all who put
your hope the Lord!

—Psalm 31:24

The Glory of God

The heavens declare the glory of God,
the skies proclaim the work of His hands.
For all of the love that God does give,
breathes life into my heart and takes full command.

This world gives us more then we feel we can take.
The shattering moments that churns us to bake.
So slowly we enter the times when we melt.
It is God's love that delivers all that is felt.

So up from the heat and rise to the best.
Take all we become and make it the test.
To climb up the peak of rocks sliding down
remembering the Lord carries the staff and
the crown.

He gave us a promise and gift in our hands.
It's tested to know if our commitment will stand.
We stand side by side without falter to fall.
For the grace that He brings lifts us up most
of all.

So on through the night may the burn be relieved,
to understand that a heartache will come to
reprieve.
We stand in true honor at loving the most.
No matter the climb, we will come through
to know;

Together forever is God's love that will be.
Standing strong in your faith will give you relief.
To never give up when all the chips are down,
onward toward heaven is walking on solid ground.

> He who has my commandments, and
> keeps them, it is he who loves Me. And
> he who loves Me will be loved by my
> Father, and I will love him and manifest
> Myself to him.
>
> —John 14:21

THE LUMINANCE LIGHTS

The moments may come when peace disappears,
the fall of the times when the heart feels the fear.
Then into the night befalls dreams turning
to fright.
So I rise from my sleep to walk around the
luminance lights.

Where do I go and where can I run.
When all around me, I am dying and undone.
To know the love leaving was never true.
I see the luminance lights shining right through.

My heart is falling into a place that I may dread,
a spinning revealing that offers up its head.
But through all the darkness that is being led.
The luminance lights show all the colors
that bled.

It brings in a peace so rich and so new.
It takes from the fire of all that is not true.
Bringing in the luminance of colors revealed.
That brings to the heart the peace to be healed.

I stand straight in front of the brilliance to be,
the luminance lights that offers to me.
Taking my heart and my soul to be free,
of marking the place that is meant to be.

So onto the day and into the night.
I rise again to walk in the luminance lights.
My heart spinning around but holds close to
the path.
Where the Lord lights my heart, I am home at last.

In all ways acknowledge Him, and He
shall direct thy path.

—Proverbs 3:6

THE RESTLESS WARRIOR

Through all the years since I was young,
I was anointed as a special one.
To choose a path given to my heart,
taken me through the war that began my start.

Trials, tribulations were had to bear,
innocence and un-clarity seemed quite unfair.
But all the while I stood up high,
for our Lord was always along my side.

I know now the reasons why,
we grow to know the scream and sigh,
I hung on hard to learn the way,
so our Lord would steer me through the decay.

For me to mold into my path,
was to learn a way to always give back.
To make the climb over mountains galore,
and slide back down to break through another
door.

Each time I never thought to make it through.
Pain erased what was done so I could start
brand new.
There is no reason, there is no rhyme.
Only growing and learning to hold the course
through the climb.

You can be used and be blessed to learn,
Your heart can open to feel others who yearn.
To know the way He makes for us,
to help get through when it becomes most tough.

Oh, how I know from the arena I came.
There is no one in this world to blame.
The plan for us is coming through the
rough, and to come out, out again not to be tough.

But love, like you are loved by Him.
Who can take your heart to feel again.
To pray and help the others to see,
a place where our Lord will set them free.

Sitting with people dying at last breath's chime,
I sing the praises so they will shine,
and only hope through what I continue to learn,
we can serve and use our hearts even from the burn.

Watch steadfast in the faith,
be brave, be strong

—I Corinthians 16:13

But Lord, be merciful to us, for we have
waited for you. Be our strong arm each
day and our salvation in times of trouble.

—Isaiah 33:2

Unseen Love

The love of our Lord is faith not seen,
by the power of His grace to believe and just be.
An instrument from above that is given to us,
to pass on the touch of His magnificent love.

Through the tests and the fire that can take
us away.
To a place that could send our faith to astray.
We hold onto the love of our Lord who
knows best.
The course of choosing right, we will come
through this test.

Then the gate opens up in a whole different way.
Your heart breaks free from the pain that once
stayed.
To a different course that's feeling the love.
Knowing it came from our Lord up above.

Does one step on in to find what it means?
Or run from the pain we remember it to be.
To gamble and risk the heart once again,
or make the decision of a new life to begin.

I look to our Lord whose love I adore.
Through the thunder of life we pull out of
the storm,
life brings in the clammier of goggling bells,
that turns into passionate favorite smells.

To risk is to gain if you're still on the path,
that takes us to heaven where eternity lasts.
So love and love well as He leads the way.
The direction of your path will come alive as
you pray.

To honor and choose the ways that please Him,
no matter what comes to take us down again.
Try in your life not to be grieved.
Our home is in heaven, we're on the road
to eternity.

> In this you greatly rejoice, though now
> for a little while, if need be, You have
> been grieved by various trials, that the
> genuineness of your faith, being much
> more precious than gold that perishes,
> though it be tested by fire, may be
> found to praise, honor, and glory at the

revelation of Jesus Christ, whom having
not seen you love. Though you do not
see him believe you rejoice with joy and
full of glory.

—Peter 1:6–8

WHAT IT MEANS TO BE HELD

There are moments we feel everything comes in
command, to want and break free of any pain we
can stand,
take it all up in prayer for His love conquers all,
that will keep you from hurting and safe from
the fall.

The peace in the moments He holds us so close,
brings tears of the joy that we all longed for
and hoped.
He takes suffering and disgrace from pain felt,
to feel all the good as we are being held

What it means to be held in the arms of our Lord,
is to break free from any harm that unfolds.
To lift up your prayers every day,
for the love of our Lord will always stay.

So often we turn to what is not best.
When the harm comes and gives us no rest.
We anguish trying to figure it all out.

In simplicity, it is God we should turn to
and shout.

"I need all your love; please hold on to me tight!
I cannot get through one more of these nights.
I am turning to you, Lord, to take it away,
and hold me in your arms where your love
will stay!"

I feel safe knowing I have been set free.
He saved me so I can finally see.
In His arms, I need not the world or myself.
To be held in God's love, my heart comes to melt

The Lord is good, a strong hold in the
day of trouble; and he knows them that
trust in Him.

—Nahum 1:7

Part III

Raise the Bar

Bend into the Wind

I gaze upon the mid-high grass that sways and bends to the wind.

The grass sways just like me gathering all the strength to begin again.

It is a choice to open our hearts and turn to the Lord our friend.

To muster up all the strength we have as we sway and bend to the wind.

Stand up tall, throw in a smile, and we show everyone our love.

Let your love shine when it becomes the most tough,

so sway even when it takes you down when bend and stand tall is a must,

sway and take all that comes, for the Lord's with you through the gust.

I gaze again to the grass that breaks and blows away.

Other strands stand and bend and seem to never break.

There are times we all take a fall when we cannot
get through.
Just like the stems of grass, we can all become
brand new.

We must hold to our faith that will keep us
feeling whole.
No matter what kind of gusts of wind, we stand
tall from the blows.
Oh! How the mighty strength that can come
from not losing hope,
like the strands of grass that bend and snap at
the howling trying to cope.

Put a picture in your mind of your very favorite
place to be.
Take yourself from the place of heck that
destroys the impossible dream.
Be the strand of blowing grass that withstands
the howling wind.
Standing tall to bend and blow coming back
into the loving again.

We all take the fall and we all get hit within.
Decide to become the mid-high grass that
bends and sways into the wind.

 AC LEVENSON

We may suffer along the way into the place that
becomes unknown.
Lift yourself up off the floor and stand tall
amongst the thorns.

You're the vessel God is hoping that no matter
you will be,
the piece of grass that lingers so that the others
may see.
Your smile and your love is the person that states
your plea.
That no matter what has happened, God's love
has set you free.

> The Lord is my strength and song, and
> he has become my salvation
>
> —Psalms 118:14

Essence of Joy

I often reflect to a place I can go,
where the joy just jumps out and the beauty
just flows.
It makes me act silly perhaps just for awhile.
But oh! how the joy brings the gladness to smile.

I drum up ideas that flow through my head,
of places I dream to take me from places I dread.
For moments, I dance around and I twirl,
that takes me from the world of sadness
that whirls.

Choose to not let anything steal your joy away.
It comes from the heart as the Lord delights in
your name.
For loving the simple things our life can bring,
to helping those needing you as your love shines
and beams.

What matters to others should matter to us.
Some stomp out the joy when it comes through
as rough.
How can the love and the joy be too much.
So keep in your heart the place thriving what must.

Bring joy to yourself so that others may know.
You can be happy even when life throws
the blows.
We choose and we grow to a place that will be,
the love and the joy that our Lord brings us
to see.

How excited a young child can be at times.
To delight over and over at something rapacious
and refined.
I watch and remember the simplicity unfold,
and delight and remember that brings back
the hope.

Let us remember the small joy of another.
To not judge or steal that that takes away
the thunder.
But rather decide to join into the delight,
that brings all the wholeness of joy that ignites.

> Blessed are the people that know the
> joyful sound: they shall walk, O Lord,
> in the light of thy countenance. In thy
> name shall they rejoice all the day: in thy
> righteousness shall they be exalted.
>
> —Psalms 89:15–16

Forgiveness

We must forgive those who hurt us and forgive
ourselves the same.
We are all born of sin, and it does not matter,
if you hurt others or were a victim of the pain.

You can become raving mad and not know what
to do.
You can throw your anger up until you
become unglued.
Ask for forgiveness and no matter what the
Lord will understand.
Because you want to change your life the Lord
will take command.

Help us all, Lord, to change our ways to take
ourselves to you.
To let go of all the suffering we hope will change
our view.
We seem to drift back to our past once we come
all the way through.
Help us, Lord, to stand strong and forget the
past that took us from you.

Give us strength to start fresh and not judge others the same.
No one on this earth should look at anyone to point as the blame.
Extend forgiveness to each other and love right from the start,
to yearn for your acceptance and to rise above the mark.

Help us to be strong and direct our path and way.
To bring a new beginning in all that shines and stays.
Take the time to stop and look at helping anyone in need.
Peel away the smoke and screens that keep us from this deed.

We all want change, and we want help in living a different life. We want your love to come into us and take us from any strife. To learn and yearn your ways, and the obedience that must be. Studying your words with prayer through this life we will finally see.

Forgive us if anything we have done will take us
far from you.
Take us up into your arms and shine your light
as we come through.
We will walk away from this day after calling
you to our side.
To lift us up and take a hold as you forgive us
another time.

It is hard in this world to stay so much like You.
We struggle just as You know as we turn our
lives in view.
To understand as You take command all we
need to come back through.
As we forgive others and ourselves, our lives will
become brand new.

> And when you stand praying, if you
> hold anything against anyone, forgive
> them, so that your Father in heaven may
> forgive you your sins.
>
> —Mark 11:25–26

Sayings That Make a Difference

Passing time is always good to look up in the sky.
To see the marvels the Lord does paint that put a twinkle in your eye.
Find the picture as you look, you'll find just what He makes.
You will feel the very closest and feel His saving grace.

> Being filled with the fruits of
> righteousness, which are by Jesus Christ,
> unto the glory and praise of God.
> (Philippians 1:11)

All the while I seem to find the reason why we are here.
The simple task we can do that makes it very clear.
To serve Him in the way that lets Him know we try.
The difference is that we have changed into a different kind.

and beside this, giving all diligence,
add to your faith virtue; and to virtue
knowledge. (2 Peter 1:5)

Up the hill up on the rocks, we climb the best we can.
Keep the pace and pray for grace and take what you can stand.
Close your eyes and see the colors you can shift
To take away the pain of life that keeps you from the drift.

But the path of the just is as the shining
light, that shines more and more unto
the perfect day. (Proverbs 4:18)

This day, I wake to start new "The Day the Lord Did Make", to take upon this day and go out into the human race.
To remember why we are here to make a mark because,
we open up and decide to change that shows our Lord His love.

If you know these things, happy are you
that do them. (John 13:17)

 AC LEVENSON

To spread the news the Lord did come is our
service most of all.
He gave His life and took our sins to set us free
from the fall.
What can we do to press forward in a way that
shows our love,
to teach those who do not know the Lord from
the heavens above.

> Herein is my Father glorified, that
> ye bear much fruit; so shall ye be my
> disciples. (John 15:8)

How beautiful the flowers with the colors full
of life.
To walk around the brilliance that makes our
hearts delight.
Yellow, green, red, and blue so many display
their worth,
magnificent is God's art display that shows His
love on this earth.

> Thou art my hiding place; thou shall
> preserve me from trouble; thou shall
> compass me about with songs of
> deliverance. (Psalms 32:7)

The passage of our Lord's words faith, hope, and love,
defines the importance why we are here,
"Our Lord reigns from above".
To never forget the words that master our cause and plan,
to know the importance that our actions follow His command.

> and now abide faith, hope, love these
> three; but the greatest of these is love. (1
> Corinthians 13:13)

Hear the ocean roar as the water lifts with tremendous spray.
The power of the ocean waves is like our lives today.
Flowing out and flowing in sometimes with great power and force.
Powerful waves can help us understand, God's hand is our true source.

> He has remembered his covenant
> forever, the word which he commanded
> to a thousand generations (Psalms
> 105:8)

THE BROKEN WING

We are born to fly, or so we think when we come
into this world,
young and bold trying to be something really
quite absurd.
I thought I'd soar above the mountains and live
according to me.
What matters most is what I thought the best
could possibly be.

But as we learn and as we grow to find the truth
of life,
the Lord opens up the path we can finally find.
I have flown up high in mighty delight not
knowing of the fall.
I could not get up because my wing was
broken off.

To fly again is what I think the best that I can do
Honoring God the healing comes, growing
starts coming into clear view
I stand up high upon the rock to spread my
wings again.

As I do, the wind kicks hard and flying starts to begin.

I descend down low, I rise up high and flow within the mark.
Only to find the broken wing I have gets hit with another dart.
So on I go to fly again seeing the beauty of our world.
Shaken up and all torn up caught back into the twirl.

I am still learning all the ways to serve God my best.
 Humble in the middle ground, soaring slowly is the test. Gravity takes me up into another realm to be reminded
Take care of the wing that once did bleed showing goodness and kindness.

Will we make it through with a broken wing unperfected with our faith;
holding strong intact, and loving God and act the best even while we ache?
How the Lord gives us grace when we just believe

   AC LEVENSON

That He died for us and rose again so we would
all be set free

Today I'm at the highest mountain looking
down and quite afraid
How can I fly with a broken wing needing
healing, can I be saved?
Take that fear and throw it out for loving God
is the road to take
If you take flight with strong faith, there is more
that can be made

Just believe and know the truth as your life turns
up to Him
He gives it all into our hearts where life can
begin again

For you are all the children of God by
faith in Christ Jesus.

—Galatians 3:26

The fruit of the Spirit is love, joy, peace,
longsuffering, gentleness, goodness,
faith, Meekness, temperance; against
such there is no law.

—Galatians 5:22–23

For by Grace you are saved through
faith; and that not of yourselves; it is a
gift of God.

—Ephesians 2:8

THE GOLDEN THREAD

I come to you, my Lord,
through all that I have known.
Like David whose heart,
was lifted up to your throne.

Just when I am on the path,
you have designed for me.
A cob in the wheel makes a turn,
that brings me to my knees.

A sudden drop in my heart falls,
Just thinking I've done wrong.
To honor you is what I do,
seeking the golden thread of you all along

I seek to stay on the golden thread,
whether it tatters, breaks, or fades,
because the thread is a better life,
then what I think to make.

I seek, I love, I fall,
to finally see the truth.
The better life I lead,

is the golden thread to You.

I try so hard to do what's right,
I change in every way.
When I blunder or do wrong,
I ask forgiveness for this shame.

But now I just know why,
it all makes since to me.
That staying on the golden thread,
sets my heart so free.

The pain of doing wrong,
comes from simply loving you.
For knowing if I fail makes the
golden thread diffused.

So hear my prayer and plea,
to take me from the wrath.
That steers me straight to you, my Lord,
down the beautiful golden path.

> The thoughts of the diligent tend only
> to plenteousness; but of every one that is
> hasty only to want.
>
> —Proverbs 21:5

 AC LEVENSON

THE SECURE GROUND

It comes in waves without warning,
to take away the light,
of promise and direction,
onto the morning light

The wave of power,
that doesn't calm the heart.
The wave that steals the light,
and shoots the fiery darts.

What strength we must give back,
to take what has been done.
Not to judge or look back,
but give nothing but our love.

Not once or twice but every time,
whoever needs to feel secure,
Is to be patient and understanding,
that brings the solid cure.

To never look back and throw the past,
but only give your love.

The support and calm will come,
with the strength and security from above.

To take the moment out,
in a very different way.
That brings the whole situation,
to a place where God remains.

It is hard not to be sad when you have
been wronged.
We must make choices that sing the tune,
So the love shows good and strong.

To you, to me, to God,
on this day, I make a pact.
That when our secured ground feels taken away,
We pray to God to bring back.

And who is he that will harm you, if you
are followers of that which is good?

—1 Peter 3:13

TERMS OF ENDEARMENT

Her wings were open to protect her nest.
The shrill of song came loud to not rest.
The mocking sound and demand to those near,
her loving wings were open without the fear.

To understand her duty calls,
to open her heart to protect them from the fall.
To love and honor the demand of what was meant,
that allowed the endearment of her heart to rest.

She watches as her little ones try to fly.
Losing one to the ground when they start to try,
she swoops down again to lift them up,
to bring them back when safety becomes tough.

She never gives up while trying to love,
the challenges come as she flies high above,
the wings swing in motion but steadfast still,
the little ones screech out with a horrible shrill.

Giving up is not what she will do.
Stopping to rest for a moment is what came
into view.

Oh! How the Lord made it for us to see,
the love in our lives keeps us from wanting to flee.

The night time comes with the calm that is felt,
as the little ones sleep under momma bird's belt.
The loud peeping is gone as she takes a sigh of relief,
that her remarkable love is the endearment she plans to keep.

> The Lord also will be a refuge for the
> oppressed, a refuge in times of trouble.
>
> —Psalms 9:9

TOW THE LINE

I was called to hold up the rock,
the bigger one that was my walk.
No matter how hard to tow the line,
the Lord has always been along my side.

I grew so fast and carried so much,
I thought my life was meant to be rough,
and then I was lifted up so high,
to tow the line was really just fine.

I rose above and started learning my life.
All through the hardships and the strife,
I grew to know that I would grow,
learning more of the Lord who loves me so

I was coming through,
When I finally realized and knew.
Discernment came so I would know,
to pray for people that helps their faith grow

In all the deep of towing the line,
the Lord was always by my side.

I always just needed to know,
the love of God and my love to show.

Stepping in to believe with my heart,
the new life I had was soon to start.
A bit of hesitation sometimes creeps in,
with time and assurance away from the spin.

To keep believing with all my heart,
the Word of God is true and would never part.
So onward, what I keep will be fine,
to tow the line was nothing to hide.

I will continue to learn and show,
my love for the Lord who helps me to know,
I am on the path that keeps me safe,
towing the line will bring me to His grace.

> God is faithful; He will not let you be
> tempted beyond what you can bear.
>
> —1 Corinthians 10:13

Part VI

When Arrows Pierce the Heart

BREAKING DAWN

It rose again like a waking tiger when memories
made were harsh.
To trust the ones we love so much can tear apart
our heart.
Hold on through the night as your thoughts and
memories flare,
for the breaking of the dawn will come and end
the night of terror.

It is always right to face the hardships that come
into our lives.
To muster up the pain inside that tries to steal
our light.
What makes us the very best that we can
always be,
is to honor God with the love that was given to
you and me.

I will walk in song as the early dawn does break.
No matter what comes that will break my
heart away.
All through the day and into the night, I will
stand upon the mound.

As the night rolls another spin, I will not fall to the ground.

The real love we will find is a true relationship with our Lord.
We try our best to represent the one who gave us life once more.
We all fall short, but continual sin is not learning along the path,
I will learn our Lord's ways to show Him how my love will last.

So humble I will claim myself and hang my head down low.
To love those who bring pain to me and pray to learn and grow.
Into the grace He gives to me, I feel it like a sweet song,
as I wake into the morning light and breaking of the dawn.

> I love those who love me, and those who
> seek me diligently find me.
>
> —Proverbs 8:17

Just Fine

I know everything is fine.
I will go along with the flow.
But the fire creeps on in,
that takes me from where I should go.

The language is spoken of a different kind,
there I stand in the mist of what I thought was
just fine.
Where I excite myself into its warmth,
till the sting drags me back into the storm.

I am baffled to say, what has happened again.
To be asked to just shove it aside,
the insecurity flares my heart falls to the floor,
but I say to myself I'm just fine.

For what better way than to gather our strength,
to give it to prayer just to know,
that any suffering in the fire we must walk,
is to come through to help us to grow.

Lonely days come and lonely nights won,
when alone in the dark I reside.

When prayer leads me on and the Lord lifts
me up,
to tell me it will be just fine.

Onward I go the work load is good,
it carries my mind to a place,
that takes what's been done to help me through,
to ease what became a disgrace.

Thank you, my Lord,
for not letting go,
you have been with me all the way,
in the dark of the night, alone and in pain,
I am fine because of your grace.

> The righteous also hold on His way, and
> he that hath clean hands shall be made
> stronger and stronger.
>
> —Job 17:9

Longing for Faithfulness

We came to a place,
where our love flew so high,
it still comes with the ache,
and deliverance with sigh.

The roll of the wave,
that thunders and shakes.
Taking all that we have,
to a slow burning bake.

The past flies right in,
from the times that did rise.
When personalities rose,
to the place of disguise.

The innocence came,
when the heart came to play,
to the place that remained,
as the life was displayed.

Together as one,
as God called it to be,
to live in this life,
as a service to Thee.

Then comes the fire,
spread through the blue sky,
the test of the love,
for eternity's time.

The test of all tests,
joining two to be one,
in the name of our Lord,
how can evil be spun?

All the love and passion,
brought forth from the love,
came the fire of dissention,
but our loving God is what was.

The anger can rise,
when insecurities coming forth.
The blend of this match,
just started to choke,
but what could it be,
that comes into sight,

 AC LEVENSON

that steals from the heart,
the horror in the night.

What happens to us,
when the horror sweeps to strike?
What comes from the past,
that hits with all its might,

The arrows that fly,
That hit straight in the heart,
How can you hang on?
Will we fall apart?

Not if you turn,
to the one who gave all.
Our Lord will do everything,
keeping the love from the fall.

So hold on so tight,
understand what's going on.
The evil will fly,
to destroy the sweet song.

Used by a power not meant to be,
it can tear a hole into a tragedy.
It comes from the darkness that nothing can last,

it is prayer to our Lord that will wash away
the past.

So onward you go,
moving forward to know,
the love that God gave,
is to have and to hold.

To go through the gates,
of heaven to show,
the Lord calls you forward,
as we all come to grow.

The truth of our hearts,
to our knees we do fall.
The passion of
our Lord
as He leads was the call.

To never let go,
to commit in the way,
to never walk out,
to never stray away,

Stay on the path,
to bring glory to Him,
no matter what comes,
the fire or the sin.

You can come through,
if you follow our Lord's lead,
to mountain tops of heaven,
the golden gates of reprieve.

Humble yourselves before God. Resist
the devil and he will flee from you, draw
close to God and he will draw close to
you.

—James 4:7

THE GRACE OF GOD

Every day in every way, my life is coming through,
the prayers, the hope, the answers
are starting to renew.

My heart was surely broken,
all the healing that was taking place,
while through the storm I ran,
to fall strong into your loving grace.

You carried me so high,
the pain just seemed to go.
There was nothing else I needed,
you made my life just glow.

Forgiveness and your love,
pulled me right on through.
To bring me to a higher place,
That I never knew.

On this day, my Lord,
thank you for being along my side.

All through the pain and suffering,
you came to be my guide.

I finally see the reason
It has become so clear,
You knew my heart was breaking
for someone to hold me near.
A miracle has happened,
to bring two empty hearts,
together and forever,
where our lives together will never part

> Dear friends, let us love one another, for
> love comes from God. Everyone who
> loves has been born of God and knows
> God.
>
> —1 John 4:7–8

Restless Heart

I lay at night so lonely in bed,
I toss and turn at that last day's dread.
Why did his love for me just slip away,
I thought the love would always stay.

On I go through the growth of loss,
upside and down and getting tossed.
But now I know, the message is clear,
the Lord is the one that knows I am dear.

Strong and steady, He knows me!
I believe my Lord would never flee.
Not a strike will be given that will raise and flare,
when insecurities worsen and our lives cannot
bear.

My pain was confronted, and prayer was the step,
you, my Lord, simply loved me the best.
So I'll hold the course as the cool wind blows,
the reins of this horse that's given me a
new course.

I will sit at the ranch, holding on to what's good,
meeting with family and friends who always understood.
The Lord knows my heart and the true way it is,
the Lord loves me regardless of being thrown into the pit.

I used to wonder, where is the love that I long to know.
The commitment of goodness that will never go,
that stays in my heart a loving good way,
to care for the feelings as it protects from the flame.

The dark cloud has left and gone away.
I have been delivered into a sweetness that seems to remain.
Now a caring and loving place where His grace is to be,
where the quiet of the room blows through with sweet harmony.

For we walk by faith, not by sight.

—2 Corinthians 5:7

THE HALLOWED GROUND

There is an ever-burning fire,
walking through the coals.
The heat intense and ever present,
burning more as the day unfolds.

Once you start down the searing path,
to take the heat with all that you can,
There is only one way you can get through,
moving forward with God is the plan.

For you, my Lord, is what we need
to carry us through the fire.
The hallowed ground you bring to us,
that turns the heat to our heart's desire.

I stand strong though the coals that burn hard.
I stand strong through the smoke and chard,
do not give up though you'll feel the pain,
stand strong and you will defeat the pouring rain.

The hallowed ground is what we seek,
that turns the burning ground into flower seeds.
Through our pain when the heat burns hot,
will keep you strong in faith toward God.

The heat will surely burn our feet,
and the smoke will choke our breath.
It is the promises He has given to us,
that will finally be our true rest.

This is the faithful saying and worthy
of all acceptation. For therefore we both
labor and suffer reproach, because we
trust in the living God, who is the Savior
of all men, specially of those that believe.

—1 Timothy 4:9–10

THE LIGHT OF GRACE

It came the day my soul did sink,
into the place this world can bring.
The utmost horror when your heart is stung,
falling into your grace, the light does come.

It springs in warmth that melts the pain.
The Lord's love comes and all does change.
It takes us out of an ongoing spin,
from the place of life where coldness is.

The light of grace I'm so grateful for.
The prayers put forth that opens the door.
To push away the harmful rays,
that will tear us down and put us away.

This I pray as your love abounds.
Still and more that your wisdom is sound.
To discern between what is right and wrong.
Following your ways and word is my true song.

All I have inside, and all I know,
abounds in me that seems to grow,
the practice and prayer in all I do,
is turning my life to what is true.

And ye are complete in Him, which is
the head of all principality and power.

—Colossians 2:10

THE LORD'S SWORD

In bitter anguish, it comes like a rain of rocks.
It takes you to the constant pain where the
enemy locks.
It strikes you down in ways to make you see.
The only place that you can go is to pray on
your knees.

The Son of man cries out, "This is not fair!"
But the Lord's message is to sharpen the sword
and prepare,
that through this test, you will come to find,
the grace of our King will be your reward at the
end of time.

So lift yourself up and hold the line.
The horror that inflicts you will be the wine.
For the strength of falling into the trap,
will take you over the mountain to never look back.

Clasp your hands and raise the sword up high.
That shows the enemy your faith will surely fly.

When the lightning strikes and the pain gets
strong;
don't fold into the old bitter song.

Take the groan inside your heart straight out.
Even though your pain wants to yell and shout.
Put on the shield of faith and lay down
your sword.
The Lord will be with you all through this horror.

The promise is in The Word our Lord gave,
that His love and peace is the only way.
In the great massacre, your face will shine,
although you may feel you're out of time.

The Sovereign Lord says again and again,
never turn to the ways of choosing sin.
Remember Job believed all to the end.
Use the Lord's words and ways to defend.

> He shall send from heaven, and save me
> from the reproach of him that would
> swallow me up. Selah. God shall send
> forth his mercy and truth.
>
> —Psalms 57:3

The Reminiscence of Love

Of risen times when the earth did shatter,
of moments golden when every moment matters,
comes all the while a shot of life,
that drives our hearts away from the optimum
fight.

For the entire world knows what we seek,
that of God and love's retreats.
But the human touch does stake our hearts,
brings the love that surely sparks.

It brings what we feel is best to be,
coming together in the sweet reprieve,
With, the smell of the finest life we see,
we come together in the love just to breath.

Taken in and out of chance,
that will honor into the best romance.
Who would have known it could go away,
 in the moments when love starts to decay.

 AC LEVENSON

Do we hold onto what we thought,
would this be the best even knowing the cost?
And knowingly never wanting to give up,
to hold the course of God's true love.

Much more than just looking back,
should we prevail all that it lacks.
To reminisce through our life or make it real,
when life here becomes the fragrance of our zeal.

So press on to know we will make our way,
to try and never go off in our mind to stray.
The world of self seems to come into play,
as we think back to what was the very best day.

> Wait on the Lord: be of good courage,
> and he shall strengthen Thine heart:
> wait, I say, on the Lord.
>
> —Psalms 27:14

TIME FOR PEACE

There is a time of peace that comes within our hearts.
It brings such sweet relief during moments with the stars.
If it could always be in tune, if it could always come to stay.
The peace in our hearts when our minds are at play.

All through the night may be the loss of someone sweet,
in searching every chance to find that time of peace.
Through coming to know, the peace will bring your glow,
turn to prayer during hard times and try to take hold.

The time of peace will come when everything is hard.
It brings the sweet relief during moments with the stars.
Take all that you can with all that you can do,

to turn around your thinking that takes away
the blues.

The purpose of our lives is when we come to
know,
we can get through to find the peace that helps
us all to grow.
The plan that is laid is understanding it is not
ours,
open up your heart and God will steer you far.

So here comes the peace just as the big wave hits,
just try to get a hold and try not to drift.
The time of peace will come after all is done
and gone,
to bring the sweet relief that brings a new
special song.

> Peace I leave with you, my peace I give
> unto you: not as the world gives, what
> I give unto you. Let not your heart be
> troubled, neither let it be afraid.
>
> —John 14:27

PART V

HOME

A King, a Queen, and a Princess

Through all the dust and mist of life,
from the dark hollows of the strife,
the good and hard times all brought new,
because of our Lord, I made it through.

On this day, I lift up my children to thee.
My Lord to help them all to see,
The love and passion they will need, even if to
bring them to their knees.

I barely got by most years.
The time just seemed to fly.
Oh! My Lord, be with all my three,
I pray you are by their side.

Will they ever see or know,
if in loving you, they will come to grow.
The pain, suffering, and life's strife,
Will not just be a way of life.

But all along, you had the plan.
Even when my children did not understand,
the day will come and they will know,
The path you laid did bring a glow.

For I have a prayer meant for all three,
A king, a queen, and a princess praying on their
knees,
that all of this in my life was meant to be.
For loving you, my Lord Brought this pathway
in my life to me.

I pray my three will come to see,
you, my loving God
hold their path and will set them free,
to forgive me for my pain and suffering.

Now therefore hearken unto me, O ye
children: for the blessed are they that
keep my ways. Hear instruction, and be
wise, and refuse it not.

—Proverbs 8:32–33

Against All Odds

I was sure the path I was on from prayer,
all the love that came through to be known.
We dove into our love with God's blessing and
grace
And our lives opened up to the growth.

We started with trust and together we prayed,
Our joy was amazing, and our passion not swayed.
The ups and downs of learning to give,
then came moments of anger that became way
too big.

I cried and we fought from a darkness that came.
The force of his anger flared up like a flame.
I did not understand when the rejection did come,
the isolation of feeling the lowest in his love.

Insecurity formed like a mountain on fire.
From his anger that came that mounted up like
a tiger.
I was struck by the hand of the one I did trust.
I lost from those moments what I thought was
his love.

We held on for a while but the drifting set in.
He felt too bound up, and I felt unloved by him.
It grew worse as the days went on by,
soon all this love just seemed to die.

I prayed and prayed as the nights set in.
A grace came in that took us out of the spin.
On my knees as I sought and wanted to get help,
all the while our hearts started to melt.

Who would have thought this could happen
with love,
a gift that came from our Lord up above.
We were carved into a place where the heart
aches in pain.
Against all odds when you lose God's grace to
the rain.

In God I have put my trust; I will not be
afraid What can man do to me?

—Psalms 56:11

Be merciful to me O God, be merciful
to me! For my soul trusts in You and in
the shadow of your wings I will make my
refuge, until these calamities have passed by.

—Palms 57:1

ERRAND BOYS

How love does stand tall when the heart comes
to play.
 Even out on the road can be made a wonderful day.
While gallivanting the stores or making the calls,
together the team is the love most of all.

To be swept up and taken when one could
not drive.
To bring in the question and time put aside,
better to take him along for my ride,
so we can be the boys that ring the tune be "By
my side".

Oh, how the day just flowed along.
Time was to kill as the errands were long.
But just for enjoyment of being the ones,
to come together in trust and growing love along.

Take in the moments to choose along the path,
to pick up and carry less in your hand,
by giving and sharing the life meant to be,
like the errand boys' love that our Lord's love
shines and sees

Blessed are the people that know the
joyful sound; they shall walk, O Lord,
in the light of thy countenance. In thy
name shall they rejoice all the day:
In thy righteousness shall they be
exalted.

—Psalm 89:15

God Bless You on Your Birthday!

May God bless you on your birthday,
with wonderful gifts and love,
from all of us who love and pray for you,
on this day, may you rise above.
May God's special blessings pour upon you,
as He lifts you up this day,
for He knows your blessings,
that always comes your way.
You always go the extra mile,
you bring such gladness in.
Your smile lifts us up when we need it most,
to those who may need help and a friend.
Perhaps I would like to let everyone know,
Just when your life began.
Being born upon this earth was one,
Being saved was the true win.
So I lift you up to our Lord above,
on this very special day,
to let you know just how you're loved,
in a very special way.

Grace be with all of them that love our
Lord Jesus Christ in sincerity

—Ephesians 6:24

HOME

Home is the place I lay my head,
into your chest at night.
Where all the hardships of the day,
seem to all take flight.

I never knew, I never thought
the way that it should be.
The love of God in our lives,
To be the unity.

There is no test that you can take,
to bring the solemn peace.
The only thing that is for real,
Is the prayer that comes to be.

So on this path we take it up,
The life dedicated to Him.
Our Lord who's given the gift to us,
to end the lonely spin.

To have and hold a special love,
that keeps us safe from the fall,

to love and cherish and trust the path,
that opens our hearts to love most of all.

Know the truth and learn the words,
our Lord brought to us all,
He suffered died and rose again,
to keep us from the fall.

Jesus gave a statement,
to be known as the golden rule.
To treat everyone with love,
and not to love our lives as fools.

As we celebrate His life,
what he gave and what He did,
to know that our Lord's suffering and death,
was His seeds of life for us to live.

So whever you go make disciples of
all nations declares the Lord Set an
example to be His disciples.

—Matthew 28:19

Trust in the LORD and do good; dwell
in the land and enjoy safe pasture. Take
delight in the LORD, and he will give
you the desires of your heart

—Psalms 37:3–5

SEEDS OF LOVE

You came to give us life.
It was a very special night.
You brought to us all my Lord,
your love for us all to love and unite.

On a very sparkling crystal night,
where all the stars shined bright.
You were born to give us life,
bathed in soft and holy light.

Let joy, love and patience,
guide you closer to his ways.
Let His spirit fill your heart,
where any pain will be erased.

The Lord brought his seeds of love,
so we would learn and grow.
The reason He came and died for us,
was to bring a new life to know.

We must change all we can,
to bring the love he gave.
The messengers we can become,
if we choose to make a change.

My Little Boo

I will not forget the day I found a tiny brown dog and lost.
Inside of a box, I was told one hundred dollars is the cost.
It looked like he was dying, underweight, and had a disease.
His little paw lifted up as if begging to say, "Take me, please!"

He melted into my arms up against my chest.
His eyes never left me as if I was his rest.
I gave the money and pushed that box aside.
I wrapped him up in a soft blanket where he tried to hide.

I never thought or ever knew the love of my dog named "Boo"
He stares while I brush my hair as if it is something new.
He protects me from anyone else that comes in close to me.
His nostrils flair up just from setting him free.

In the late of night, he snuggles up as I pat his head.
He knows for sure his deeds been done, and it's time for bed.
He loves people now; he learned to trust from security taken long ago.
The greeter is the name he is called with confidence that glows.

I leave for work so early, he knows just when the time comes.
He runs from the room as I reach for the door, he becomes undone.
I love my little Boo whose confidence I've raised sky high.
He believes with all his heart and loves with all his might.

Boo knows when someone's bad or would hurt him in anyway.
I've seen him run under the bed sensing trouble might come to stay.
It does not happen too often, but when it does, I know,
to listen to his reaction and insure him I love him so.

 AC LEVENSON

My little dog named Boo has come to be the glue.
Watching him grow, learn, and explore all things new.
I will stroll out to the porch as he follows me all the way.
Oh! How I know my Boo is always here to stay.

These things have I spoken unto you,
that my joy might remain in you, and
that your joy might be full.

—John 15:11

The Journey of our Love

We met at the top of the hill,
when our eyes met for the very first time.
You glanced with a smile and a gleam,
that I saw from the deep of your eyes.

God was the one in control,
for you waited for such a long time.
For me, I was scared but elated,
to feel the love of the true sweet divine.

The friendship just started to grow,
that helped me to see and to know,
you showed that your heart was the glue,
that could carry the love coming true

Christmas eve I came in to know,
the gift you gave to me in a box with a red bow,
that stole my heart over to know your love
was sound,
oh, how I love that red flannel nightgown!

It grew and grew this love of ours,
the love of ours reached to the stars.
We made a commitment to one another,
to love cherish and honor each other.

Under our Lord, we committed,
our wedding was a gift and God driven,
to know each other more every day,
and connect in a whole new way.

I cannot wait until I get home each night,
so you, my dear sweet love, can hold me so tight.
The night just seems to go by so fast,
how I love when we know and trust our
loves path.

How did this happen? we seem to always ask,
the miracle of our lives coming together at last.
You,
waiting so long to share and to love,
me, not knowing love of man who loved our
Lord above.

I remember the moments before I walked down
the aisle.

The breeze of the sun through the trees made
me smile.
All around was the love of friends and family
coming together.
To share what we found and to believe is forever.

Onward we go growing older together.
Knowing our time is special and favored.
For God brought to us a gift to love one another,
to put Him first and pray with each other.

Together on our knees we lift up to Him.
The love we show each other that will give our
Lord a grin.
For the power of our faith with the path He
gave to us,
we will hold in our hearts to always remember
how to love.

To put our own selfishness aside,
and give to each other the solid and refine.
Actions to show just how much we adore,
the blessings poured upon us that opened up
our door.

 AC LEVENSON

To find that the path relieves the heart at rest,
to know the love is truly the test.
The hardships, temptations, disappointments of life,
will dissipate forever in the eternity of life.

I love you, and you promised to cherish me all our lives.
You hold in my heart the place no one else could find.
Your love is the air that I breathe in each night.
I feel your every move that has taken away the fright.

I want you to know with all of my soul.
You take away my breath that helps me unfold,
the truth in the path where our Lord came to us,
to show you and I the gateway to true love

Love each other deeply
with all your heart

—1 Peter 1:22

THE MAGNIFICENT MAN

He never walked in with ego or charm.
The way of his manners was wholesome with
regard,
his confidence strong without raising his flag.
The moment to recall was the happiness he had.

Inside of his being brought forth with a smile.
Knowing the pain he was under, never showing
the vile.
For his voice rose with solemn pure strength
from his heart,
the love and passion created from God.
He shares with great calm the pain inside his
soul.
His talents so noticed and his art to behold.
I cannot fathom ever being without,
the love and the laughter he shares all about.

His love for the Lord shines and his passions fly.
I feel the light he holds deep inside.
Where I know I must be when he needs me
to show,
the one that will love him and helps us to grow.

A magnificent man I know that he is.
Without his love and his touch, it would be hard
to live.
Onward he goes into the day,
My man is leading our lives all the way

I lift our lives to You, my Lord.
For any pain and suffering he may hold.
Bring to him the gift of your grace,
that will bring to him comfort and less hurt
and pain.

The magnificent man knows it's not about what
he owns.
But the simple things of life that we can withhold,
to honor and live in obedience to you,
where life may mean suffering to begin coming
through.

> Delight thyself also in the Lord; and he
> shall give thee the desires of your heart

—Psalms 37:4

THE SHIMMERING KNIGHT

Out from the battle, he walks in very tall.
A quiet strength recognized most of all.
A humble way for all to behold,
that drew in the crowd of the noble one to
be bestowed.

The one with the light that we hold so dear,
it is when the sight of the shimmer comes clear,
to come to a place where we all want to be,
when the shimmering knight shines because he
was set free.

For he chooses the path that is the hardest grade.
Following God is the choice that he will make.
He is clear in his mind, and his heart
shines through.
For the choices he makes in turning his life to
what's true.

Out of the wreckage, this world brings to our life.
To change who we are to become fully alive.
When hardships from the battle come clear to
our hearts,
standing tall for what's right will set him apart.

 AC LEVENSON

So in from the battlefield of life's heavy grime,
Walks in a different look where you can shimmer
and shine,
to take on the world in a whole different fight,
to lift your head to show forth at the highest high.

For the shimmer of the knight who shines strong
in God's hands,
is fighting the battles in a way of true command,
to those all around who want to step into
the realm,
for commitment that will take lead to the helm.

Shimmer on, my knight, no matter what comes
your way,
 your honor and your humbleness are the prayers
being laid.
To show when it's hard and the pain seeps
on through,
you shimmer and shine as the knight God has
called you to.

> For the Lord God is a sun and shield;
> The Lord will give grace and glory; no
> good thing will he withhold from them
> that choose to walk uprightly.

—Psalms 84:11

Beams of Light

I saw the beams of light shine down,
to the place I know where love is bound.
The peace, warmth, and solitude,
I knew he would be carried up into.

The prayers were all up for him.
My dad who always showed a grin,
his pain soon gone, forgetfulness too,
on the way to the home of heaven so new.

Where you, my Lord, will take a hold,
to bring him through the gates of gold,
where everyone he new went first,
he will see again where happiness will burst.

I felt the warmth of you going home.
It gave to me much more than hope.
I know some day the link will come together,
all of us brought up united again forever.

So on this day, just know we are all here,
my dear sweet dad, you will lose all fear.
Having you close and hearing your voice,

will be remembered forever where our hearts
rejoice.

The memories of you stand tall in our minds,
the laughter, the good times, and love of all time.
It is you we hold near and will never let go,
until we meet again, in the new life of heaven
to behold.

Fathers to not exasperate your children;
instead, bring them up in the training of
the Lord.

—Ephesians 6-4

PART VI

DARING TO DREAM

FORWARD TOWARD HOME

We come to our Lord and our life starts to change,
the moments we thought this life was our gain.
But truth comes to be the life of our path,
that turns our life over to a faith that will last.

Onward and forward, we move at a pace,
that changes our lives in the mist of our face.
It changes the colors and hues in our thoughts,
as our Lord's words and ways are what is
being taught.

Who would have known from when we
were young,
the Lord had our path waiting for us just to come.
We were thrown into this world to doubt and
know pain,
so we pushed all the love far away to sustain.

Only to find it can only get worse,
our lives upside down and starting to hurt.
The home that we seek is truly not here,
heaven is the place you will have no more fear.

The growing in us starts to open us up.
We beg for forgiveness and change what we must.
For down on our knees in repenting our ways,
is the secret of growing toward home in
God's grace.

Choose to round the corner of leaving your fears.
Gain strength in your faith as your life
becomes clear.
All around you will find that your path given
by God.
Was the learning and drawing close to the
heavens above.

Through the fire and the hardships we all come
to know,
will help us to gain a new meaning to grow.
We want and we need our faith to succeed,
forward towards home is the gateway to peace.

For the wages of sin is death; but the
gift of God is eternal life through Jesus
Christ our Lord.

—Romans 6:23

 AC LEVENSON

Our Patch of Blue

There is a place I go that makes me feel so new.
I lie down upon the long green grass and look
up to my patch of blue.
It follows all the shadowing of white clouds
to behold.
The billow of colors and hews of blue where
glory is bestowed.

Sometimes I walk sometimes I run to find my
patch of blue.
Each time I go, the colors change just like the
way we do.
I found a place where I can go that brings such
a peace,
the colors of blue come in the night even while
I sleep.

Together we will come to know it matters if
we care.
To encourage, love, and speak the language with
a positive flair.
The love will grow and always last because we
run the race,

of getting through to understand in setting up our pace.

This love of ours gains the course of moving forward that will be,
in getting through all that we do so we will be set free.
We found our love and found our life in a beautiful place to see.
The patch of blue has all the hues to never doubt but be relieved.

On this course, we move together walking or running this path.
Where the patch of blue that we see will always and forever last,
To bring us to our knees each day in honor of our Lord,
the faith the hope the love that will keep us on the course.

> Let the husband render unto the wife
> due benevolence: and likewise Also the
> wife unto the husband.
>
> —1 Corinthians 7:3

THE AMBASSADOR FOR CHRIST

None of us are perfect; we know that being born
of sin.
It matters most to please our Lord that is the
true win.
Come to know His word and ways and what we
should say and do,
if we close the door to our faith, we could
surely lose.

We are struggle trying with all we have to stay
away from sin.
It means we wear a banner that sings the
winning hymn.
But all the while I must admit if I fail in any way,
I cannot sleep, my insides hurt, and I'm on my
knees to pray.

Forgive me if I've lost sight of being the best in
every way.
You matter more importantly in everything I do
each day.

It is our faith we show forth when we are strong enough to learn.
Your word and ways matter so much, living for you is what we yearn.

What does it mean to serve if we do not follow the words you sent.
To adhere the true wisdom in a way our love for you is meant.
What leaders can we be if weakness becomes our call.
We turn wrong showing nothing as we choose to constantly fall.

I ask for you to teach me as I learn not to repeat mistakes,
To take serious the ways that could bind me if I become a disgrace.
I pray to stand as an ambassador to do the very best I can,
to honor you and show my love and become your biggest fan.

To never take for granted what matters most to you.

And strive to move on boldly in the lane that shows I'm true.
Oh! My Lord, I love you with all my heart and soul.
Please help me as your ambassador; as I learn to grow.

> Know then in your heart that as a man
> disciplines his son, so the Lord your
> God disciplines you. Observe the
> commands of the LORD your God,
> walking in his ways and revering him.
>
> —Deuteronomy 8:5–6

THE CABIN ON THE HILL

We grew into the love we had; our house was modest and cute.
She grew a garden in the patch and made light boxes with jewels.
 Our times were spent outside; our cabin covered from the sun.
Hot chocolate and hot cider we drank on our chairs just for fun.

Years gone by, more in love, seeing simpler things of life,
watching her pick from our herb garden to make us soup with spice.
Oh! How these days have flown by bringing tears to me,
not wanting to go back when life was harder to see.

It is clear what we went through to finally live at rest.
Beneath the trees in front of our cabin where I like it best.

I watch her as she walks around in the ankle
skirt with stripes.
Cute as a button and still is, but now she tries
to hide,
the lines upon her face, she loves to wear her hat.
I have come to how much our love became the
perfect match.
To honor God who gave to us a future and
the hope,
to grow in love by each other's side, knowing we
would cope.

We love our house that looks out from our porch
to see,
we both want to grow together to eternity.
I watch the wind blow her grey hair fly up high,
a peace comes that brings relief with our love
and a sigh.

And they said, Believe on the Lord Jesus
Christ, and you will be saved, you and
your house hold

—Acts 16:31

THE GREEN PASTURES CALL

I sit in a calm just thinking of you,
wherever I am, in the traffic or in crowds.
A mist from the air comes blowing right through,
I dream of green pastures where colors turn new.

I step out to have a warm drink on the porch,
while the mist from the fog comes up from
the north.
I watch as the cows come up from the hill.
I dream of the calm in the green pastures so still.

A cabin of wood while the old pipe stove warms,
to the smell of the pine near the old sweet
wood barn.
Never a moment like this could I hope,
to dream of the quiet green pastures that slope.

On through the day the hectic life comes in,
the paperwork high the phones ringing in a spin.
All the while as I work in a place that
screams noise,
I glance in my mind and the true life deploys.

The pastures of green come clear to my mind,
the thought of my love when we have made the
good climb.
To build the foundation that brings us to
what's real,
where the green pastures call is the peace that
we feel.

> And let the peace of God rule in your
> hearts, to which also ye are called in one
> body; and be ye thankful
>
> —Colossians 3:15

THE LONG WOOD PORCH

I walk along the long wood porch where the smell of night time grows.
The view from here is green with grass along the creek that flows.
All through this land is peace from God where traffic never comes.
The only sound and feel are the breeze from the grass and the sun.

I wake each day to hear the birds just chirping their mighty song.
As the warmth seeps through the window pane, I see the rays of light that's begun.
I grab this moment on the long wood porch where I sit for a moment on the rail,
all to capture every view from the porch as the morning winds do sail.

Our Lord does bring the simple life when we stop to look around.
Like the smell of the long wood porch bringing fragrant and squeaky sounds.

Take in the moments from within your day to find the simple life,
the Lord will bring just what you need from sounds, smells, and sights.

The views and smells from the long wood porch are so wonderful to me,
as I take it all in with a smile just knowing what is to be.
For the plan He laid in every way is to grow stronger each day,
it is the simple life in our Lord where I have chosen to stay.

When you hear the noise or in the place of uncertainty Think of the place where your life can grow toward eternity Your heart will find that moment of sweet peace along the path
Our Lord will bring you into the place where your life's joy will always last

> I will instruct you and teach you in the
> way that you will go; I will guide you
> with mine eyes.
>
> —Psalms 32:8

And He will teach us of His ways, and
we will walk in His path

—Isaiah 2:3

Night Noise

I hear the tone in the night,
a quiet snore to my delight.
You're with me now as it should be,
I hear your noise as I try to sleep.

A smile appears upon my face
late into the night,
Just when I start to fall asleep,
your noise turns into a different kind.

I feel your heart beat,
I breathe your air,
The smell of you surrounds me,
As I look at you and stare.

In the night, your noise does light
a brilliant kind of hew,
I love the noise I hear,
because I know it's you.

When you are gone, I cannot sleep,
the noise, I long for is now not a peep.
I lay awake just to think,
your night noise fills me to the brink.

In every way and in every thought,
how our love is growing and being taught.
In every moment that loves does bring,
the night noise I hear is you next to me.

When you and I come close to know,
our passion flies into another fold.
The noise of you just keeps in me,
the loving thoughts of your company.

To feel your heartbeat
As I turn to you and stare,
The love that surrounds me
As I breathe in your air.

The night noise brings it clear to me,
the love we share so endlessly.
So when your noise does rise again,
I know my love the night noise wins.

And beyond all these things, put on love,
which perfect for unity

—Colossians 3:14

 AC LEVENSON

WHERE ANGELS WALK

All along the path I feel the ache,
when the night turns frail and I can't sleep.
Then the call comes from the night and steers
my plight,
while around me, I feel the spirit of the
angels breathe.

Pick yourself up in the world where life can hurt.
When the love and respect can leave and
get worse.
 Where we should live and join into harmony.
Think of the good and all that it can be.

The air picks up when the strife just spins,
all the love moves out and just moves back in.
When the worst gets worst and knocks you to
your knees.
Think of the good to be so you can feel the
angels breathe.

The angels follow and protect our path.
They are sent to help and give a peace that lasts.
When we show the Lord what we need to help,
our prayers are answered and His grace is felt.

There is a war on our earth today.
The simple truth; turn to the Lord and pray.
This will surround your house where protection
is laid,
and you will know in your heart the angel's mark
was made.

     AC LEVENSON

WHERE THE COLORS GROW

I am in my garden these days and nights
thinking of family and friends with a
commitment in sight.
But all the while I have come to know,
the love of our Lord will never go.

You, my Lord, bring sweet relief.
You rest my heart and come into me.
I lay amidst this beautiful land,
where the wild flowers grow and take command.

The brilliance of color is what I see,
although I question what is meant to be.
your plan, I know, is better than mine,
so I'll take a strong hold of the vine.

I pass this on for others to know,
if the changes come so does the growth.
Sometimes the path is hard to understand,
It is the Lord who holds our special plan.

I watch the wild flowers grow up and old.
They fall apart some turn to mold.
But through the seasons, the beauty returns,
the beautiful colors I will always yearn.

I lay beneath the gold and blue,
the yellow surrounds the bright white hues.
I'll reach into the colors that He has made,
and think of heaven and the pearly gates.

> Trust in the Lord with all you heart; and
> lean not on your own understanding. In
> all ways acknowledge him, And he shall
> direct thy path.
>
> —Proverbs 3:5–6

My Home Is Heaven, I'm Just Traveling Through

My home is heaven, I'm just traveling through.
God is the reason knowing all good is what's true.
For love is the call as we walk through our lives,
to help one another in the need and demise.

People need people and love that depends,
on giving and helping each other to mend.
For God's love is calling and opens to see,
turning all that we have over with faith to believe.

While we work and we play or we just barely
get by,
we live here for purpose where grace grows in
our lives.
Remind yourself we are here for a very short while,
we are traveling through this world on a
temporary trial.

Oh how the peace of grace flows through my veins,
of God's love and glory that helps me sustain,
in living this life to the glory of Him,
is to know that heaven is the destination and
purpose live.

My home is in heaven, let me not forget,
leaving our earth to the place that is meant,
where peace, love, and joy will raise high in
my heart,
to be with our Lord through the gates with
the stars.

We cannot forget we are just traveling through,
to love one another and help those who
never knew,
that God is the way and the truth and the light,
to carry us home to the place of pure delight.

Starting this day, remember your gift,
To use what you have to the goodness to live,
to spread the good news of why we are here,
and leave at the doorstep your moments of fear.

 AC LEVENSON

Yes, we are of good courage, and we
would rather be away from the body and
at home with the Lord.

—2 Corinthians 5:8

But our citizenship is in heaven, and
from it we await a Savior, the Lord Jesus
Christ, who will transform our lowly
body to be like his glorious body, by the
power that enables him even to subject
all things to himself

—Philippians 3:20–21

Part VII

Sharing the Light

THE CHURCH ON THE HILL

A day came along when I lost all my heart,
where will I go to find a church for my new start,
the Lord's always been the part of my life,
Fellowship, Worship, and His word take away
the strife.

The message was clear when I was offered to see,
the church on the hill that was meant to be.
Where neighbors, friends, and family alike,
come together in love learning the Lord's ways
of life.

The light and the gleam of the word taught
with passion,
the caring and knowing what is wise with
impression.
That takes up the soul to wanting much more,
teachings of truth and the word of our Lord.

Higher and higher to where we should be,
we are learning the word and how the Lord set
us free.
To come into terms we never thought or knew,
the church on the hill sets our sights in clear view.

Here comes the praise of another new song.
Played by our pastor on just how we long,
for more of this teaching that seems to undo,
the ravel of our lives when we can come unglued.

So as we all gather to find the true path,
to learn of our Lord so our hearts can relax,
the blessing is here as the moments just mold,
the church on the hill is where God's grace unfolds.

Now we ask you, brothers and sisters,
to acknowledge those who work hard
among you, who care for you in the Lord
and who admonish you. Hold them
in the highest regard in love because
of their work. Live in peace with each
other.

—1 Thessalonians 5:12–13

The Flower Fields

Among the most beautiful days,
is walking along the path,
that fills your heart so endlessly,
of a beauty that will last.

Of roses red and yellow,
where green and white blend in,
to orchards, daffodils and sunflowers,
around to another bend.

The days pass by and the months move on,
the flowers all lose their bloom,
it turns to dirt and mud,
as the flower fields turn to gloom.

The stems turn to sticks and weeds
all the flowers turn to dust,
Just looking all around,
turns the heart to mush.

Just like what life can do,
to make us feel the gloom,
the seasons change around again,
that brings us back to be renewed.

Months have passed and around the bend,
I pass the flowers back in bloom,
flowers rise again and sway
colors to a beautiful tune

I move forward into the path life has brought
to me,
not always will the season
bring happiness and sweet relief

but through the turns and valleys
you will come upon to know
like the flowers coming back to bloom
the simple joy of life will bring your glow

> The hoary head is crown of glory, if it be
> found in the way of the righteousness.
>
> —Proverbs 16:31

THE GLIMMER OF LIGHT

In all the work that must be done,
we scurry through our day.
To accomplish all is just a must,
the importance is the grace being is laid.

To bring ourselves to a different beat,
that leaves those hearts at rest,
to bring a newness to those around,
That reflects the reason of test.

So sing the song while the rough sets in,
and change the way it comes,
into the place of solid ground,
where love has just been spun.

I see it clear all in my mind,
as I take it on this day.
The brilliance of the toil that comes,
and the glimmer of light that stays.

For in this light, I see my place,
That takes me to my faith,
To understand the importance of life,
In a very different way.

I thank the Lord with all my heart
who gives me everything,
That teaches me to be the best,
the best that I can be.

The glimmer of light I see so clear
To guide my way this day,
To pull me through to lift me up,
to give in every way.

How I love the shine so bright
I long for it to stay,
But on this road, it comes and goes
the feel of His saving grace.

And beside this, giving all diligence,
add to your faith virtue; and to virtue
knowledge

—2 Peter 1:5

The Hills Are Alive

Even on a raining day, the hills of green are in view.
Moisture throughout the stretch of land puts my sight in clear view.
To gaze upon the wet green grass of hills that penetrates in ways,
that takes you to another land with the hills that never sways.

I run with joy going up and down over what life brings so sweet,
a rumbling deep within my soul that nothing could ever beat.
Just look around your head held high and see the beauty come alive,
that draws you close with baited breath to know you will survive.

The hills alive with sound of music you can hear from far away.
The orchestra sounds with a special flow of never wanting to stray.

So in this moment on these grounds, a secret
is revealed,
the rolling green not often seen is what will
make you feel.

God did make it all for us so always lift your eyes.
To find the places in our world that brings the
hills alive.
To learn the word of our Lord that shows what
is revealed.
To muster up the only place you'll find the
beauty of the hills.

And you shall rejoice in the Lord, and
glory in the Holy One of Israel.

—Isaiah 41:16

 AC LEVENSON

THE MORNING MOON

The days are hard
The weeks are long
The night just slips away
Then came the morning,
with all the glory,
That opened my heart to pray.

A new day was born
when all felt lost,
the light still flickered through,
As I looked up into the sky
I saw the morning moon.

When all of life
is hard to hold
the dust and sand shift on in,
hold strong unto your faith,
knowing the darkness is the fight from within.

Look to dispel
The hardest times,
as a yearning to come through,
just as our Lord who suffered for us,

brought us back to be renewed.
Look to the thoughts
of simple sight,
that will melt the pain away.
That will catch our eyes,
to understand why,
we must wipe away the days dismay.

The morning moon seldom comes,
but only now and then.
It goes away when morning comes as life begins
again.

Let us hold fast the profession of our
faith without wavering; (for he is faithful
that promised).

—Hebrews 10:23

THE NOON DAY SUN

No matter the time of day that will come,
the warmth surely comes from the noon day sun.
It shines from the top between all the trees,
that fills up your soul that brings such a peace.

Onward and upward, our world calls us to,
knowing and holding the hardships blown
through,
but always no matter how coldness comes in,
the warmth and the faith are what surely will win.

I lay in the meadow behind the old truck,
the rusts and shimmers of lighting that struck.
Lying down in the grass feeling safe and
with peace,
All in my mind while thinking love is the need.

It's all up to us to come to the place.
Where opening your heart will find peace and
His grace,
to take all you can and take all that is done,
where the cold and the rain can become warm
from the sun.

Here in the moments where taking hold of
the day,
brings in a gladness and love in a very special way.
The rays of the sun come shimmering on through,
as my heart starts to rise and shines the light in
clear view

I choose in my life to take hold of my thoughts,
and carry the load as our Lord carried the cross.
To look and distain all the pain that comes
through,
as the rays of the sun shine a whole different view.

With long life will I satisfy him, and
show him my salvation.

—Psalms 91:16

 AC LEVENSON

The Returning Joy of Love

I often look back at what passion we had.
The missing of you were moments of sad.
The commitment to belong to our Lord from above,
was the joy in the life that mounted up in our love.

Then came the growing and learning to trust,
trust was the word that my heart entered as a must.
New and broken being unclear and unsure,
the world I moved down to wanting acceptance not unstirred.

The growing and learning the importance of love,
to follow when broken to forgiveness was tough.
To remember back when your eyes met with mine,
the passion we had when our hearts were entwined.

What changes the course of our lives when
we grow?
Together we still want and need the passion
to know,
the trust and respect that become good and true,
will bring in the joy like when the love becomes
new.

To remember what is important to each of us,
as we move forward and up away from the dust.
To understand not demand what it is we
both need,
together we go to our Lord on our knees.

To gather strength that will set us apart,
to lift up newness that takes care of our hearts.
To love one another as we become one,
as the returning of love shines like the sun.

Onward we learn and grow just to know,
 to never give up and keep our passions to glow.
To gaze across the room to feel what is warmth,
that will comfort and keep us away from
the storms.

 AC LEVENSON

I love you so much, so please know on this day,
our lives have merged through all the growing pains.
You and I have a commitment that we will always see,
the returning of joy and love is what will always be.

> Likewise, husbands, live with your wives
> in an understanding way, showing honor
> to the woman as the weaker vessel, since
> they are heirs with you of the grace of
> life, so that your prayers are answered.
>
> —1 Peter 3:7

THE SOURCE OF IMPACT

Inside my heart, a peace comes from deep within.
The busy life and clanking noise that can pull us into sin,
pressing forward to choose the path our Lord calls us to,
will take the impact from the fall and bring us into life that is new.

You may want to make a significant impact in our world today,
the true impact that we can make is living our lives to pray,
showing forth a different call that sets us apart from the rest,
well recognized and criticized for loving God is the real test.

In the secret of His presence how my soul delights to hide.
How precious are the lessons when Jesus is by my side.
As endless as God's blessings so should my praises be,
for all His daily goodness that flows unceasingly.

The impact of His love is all I want to seek.
To change my life and ways to reflect and show
the real me,
All to the glory of the One who gives us so
much more,
will just unfold to stand out because I'll be
the source,

who stands up high and to be the one of strength,
who gave to me the confidence to fill me to
the brink,
I'd rather be a Christian than to hear one
merely talk,
I'd rather see his actions and behold ones
daily walk.

So take up the cross the Lord has said
be my disciples follow me and be led.
Take it up with a loving heart and you will
surely see,
you're the example for our Lord on how to act
and how to be.

> Then Jesus explained: "My nourishment
> comes from doing the will of God, who
> sent me, and from finishing his work
>
> —John 4:34

WEATHERING HEIGHTS

The Lord has ways in our lives to steer us to
a place,
that makes sense as we seek to find His
loving grace.
Along it comes to help the heart the one who's
called to be,
the friend that gives that extra touch of
exceptional novelty.

With long years passed and age set, we learn
wisdom's ways,
to go through the fire that is learned to change
and never sway,
this will bring into our lives the glow of
someone new,
to bring a friend that helps the heart in God's
fashion that is true.

The twin trees stand tall up on the hill that have
grown for many years.
The scares and marks that make it strong when
the wind blows away the fears,

but then the day comes in at last as the sun
comes shinning through,
to the beauty at rest when the foundation and
roots grab hold into view.

The beauty is what we must see when the storm
comes in at will.
Hold on when digging deep into the ground,
while your heart is trying to feel.
To grow old in truth is learning what God's path
really is,
to take it on no matter what life brings, when we
start to spin.

A clear day arrives up on top of the hill when
you see the twin old trees' growth.

Weathering they are but beauty is seen, like the
memories taken back from the smoke,
to learn from prayer that the Lord is true and
brings to us a hope,
so we can stand strong like the strength of the
trees that have weathered and will always cope.

Weathering heights is the climb we must make
to find the sweetest relief.

Grabbing hold to the importance of life, as we learn and heal from scares of defeat.
Knowing the friends who stand by our side will help us get through hard times.
Are the friends that we keep and count on one hand as God's path becomes clear and refined.

Let love be without dissimulation, abhor that which is evil, cleave to that which is good.
Be kindly affectionate one to another with brotherly love. in honor preferring one another, this is all understood.

> Let love be without hypocrisy. Abhor
> what is evil. Cling to what is good.
> Be kindly affectionate to one another
> with brotherly love, in honor giving
> preference to one another
>
> —Romans 12:9–10

 AC LEVENSON

Part VIII

Hand in Hand

Best Friends

Times come a changing when life moves along,
to places remembered like an old country song,
then out of the blue comes the moment that shows,
a friend you come closer to that begins to know,
the truth of your heart and way that you are,
you feel a gentle tugging as you gaze to the stars,
just to know what's been captured is real and makes sense,
to stop for a moment to sit upon that fence.

No hurry or scurry or drag to the line.
Just a tug to the heart that feels so divine.
The knowing of truth with acceptance of joy,
just who we are without judgment that never employs.

So important to the one that understands who you are,
as the growing and knowing becomes the strength from afar,
like the old oak tree that grows and withers as time goes,

are the friends that become the family that never
let's go.

You and I came to know the important part
of life,
to understand the heart which takes us from
the strife.
The hope growing in strength to the life that
becomes new, is the purpose of our lives that
brings strength in clear view.

For knowing is the growing of who you really are,
to be unafraid of saying just what comes into
the heart.
No matter what the moment brings it's all in
tune to know,
God has brought a purpose of two friends who
have come to grow.

In strength of God who brings into us the light.
That shines in the moments we misunderstand
the fight.
Then growing and the holding onto what makes
it right,
our Lord who died for us to take our path to
eternal life.

In the holding and the purifying of our souls
obeying the truth,
our Lord loved us to love one another to help each
other through.
For I know the plans I have for you declares the
Lord on high,
to prosper and not harm us as we scurry through
this life.

Oh, my mighty Lord, I put this prayer up for
my friend,
that all the words you have given will raise him up
to mend.
This will give him strength that will take him to
that place,
where his life will raise above the mark because
of your loving grace.

Put on then, as God's chosen ones, holy
and beloved, compassionate hearts,
kindness, humility, meekness, and
patience, bearing with one another and,
if one has a complaint against another,
forgiving each other; as the Lord has
forgiven you, so you also must forgive.
And above all these put on love, which

binds everything together in perfect
harmony.

—Colossians 3:12–14

For I know the plans I have for you
declares the Lord, plans to proper you
not harm you, plans for hope and a
future.

—Corinthians 13:13

Love Remains

I stand at the ocean to watch the waves at the shore,
thoughts of you swarms me and fills me once more.
an ache comes at moments the waves crashing occurs,
to take the fulfillment of wanting only to be heard.

To understand the reasons of heartache and pain,
is only the season with much to be gained.
For times the calm comes even late in the night,
like the ocean when resting and calm is at sight.

We hold to the goodness with love in our hearts,
where nothing will ever take our love apart.
Although through the weakness the ache does appear,
we move in a direction where we lose all our fears.

I see you so clearly in my mind when you're gone.
I need you so dearly for it is you that I long.
I hold you so closely and feel that you're strong.
To help me through anything this life brings along.

To have and to hold from this day forward,
a meaning inside me just seems to go onward.
The commitment of sharing the good with
the bad,
so onward we go into all that we have.

There is nothing I want more than you by my side
To know you and love you with memories in sight
The pictures so clear now our love will take flight
Into the new life to enjoy with the Lord by our side

> Nevertheless let every one of you in
> particular so love his wife even as
> himself; and the wife see that she
> reverence her husband.
>
> —Ephesians 5:33

My Heart's Desire

Someone has come into my life,
from a very heartfelt prayer.
It opened up to my surprise,
The glory and despair.

More than strong our hearts do beat,
with moments turned to you,
we did defeat our tragic pasts,
the never-ending lowered boom.

My life has been in serving You,
and you have blessed me so,
the love, the grace, and protection,
that have made my life just glow.

You've given me so much, my Lord
loving you is all I do,
but with all my heart, I would like
sharing my life in service to you.

Please hear my heart when I say
I know you are aware,
but lift him up and give him grace,
to take him from the glare.

It settles in this world of ours the pain,
the loss, our drive,
that could even bury us,
that would steal your grace and light.

My choice, my Lord, if you will allow
is to be along his side,
to be the wife that God does see,
while you lead us as our guide.

He loves you so, just as you know,
please hear my heart's desire.
We will to be one, for a new life spun,
we will make it through the fire.

So hear my heart about his loss
and put him in the place,
where he will climb the mountain tops,
to receive your blessings and grace.

For the Lord God is our sun and shield.
He gives us grace and glory.

—Psalms 84:11

 AC LEVENSON

My Sweet Lord

You fill my soul with such delight.
The song is heard inside my mind.
My heart fills in sweet refrain,
the love from you that still remains.

I see the shine of you at night,
I feel the gleam of your love in sight,
it takes from the realm of tough,
to remind me again of your sweet love.

It is you who takes me from being down.
To not give up on life when pain comes around,
to hold the line even when it's shred,
to never lie down to the blows of dread.

I will wake each day to your delight.
I will hold my love to the highest high!
I will not hymn and haw at the day that breaks,
and rather make your word my only stake.

Will I rise above when the sword does fly.
Am I strong enough to hold making moments
delight,

into you, my Lord, who shows me how,
to move ahead from the perilous pestilence prow.

I know the truth inside my soul.
Your sweet love for me that never let's go.
How favored I feel when your grace comes strong,
to lift me up and move me along.

Your protection I need in every way.
Your grace I pray will always stay.
I try so hard to be the best,
with you, my Lord, I can finally rest.

> Surely He shall deliver you from the snare of the fowler and from the perilous pestilence. He shall cover you with His feathers, and under His wings you shall take refuge; His truth shall be your shield and buckler.
>
> —Psalms 91:3–4

     AC LEVENSON

THE DIVINE ROMANCE

I dreamed of a time when the love would come in.
That breath of fresh air when that romance begins.
The only knowing of what is so sweet and
so good,
where nothing else could ever be misunderstood.

The learning and churning of everything new,
like smelling the flowers when they are first
in bloom.
Lying on the grass staring up at the sky,
the divine romance where nothing else flies.

Hearing the voice while you're madly at work,
remembering the moments together that keeps
you alert.
Oh! How can it be that everything so new,
like a child first sees the brilliance of colors
and hues.

Isn't it lovely as the time rolls on by,
the romance still twinkles in growth while abide,
in nothing simpler than love's perfect toast.

when you see your life changing and the future
to boast.

Then in true time the real growth does come.
To understand the love and romance and fun, is
giving and taking and not giving up!
but to carry the romance in God's true love.

Remember how divine the moment was,
then came the learning and growing because,
just like our faith we grow and we learn,
so keep up the romance and hold to the stern.

Drive at the helm and steer as the team.
Show each other true loyalty so others may see.
That God is at work as husband and wife beams,
the divine romance brings back the truest gleam.

This is what the Sovereign Lord says:
Look I am going to put breath into you
and make you live again!

—Ezekiel 37:5

 AC LEVENSON

THE RED FLANNEL NIGHTGOWN

Upon the eve of a special night,
was to seek a nightgown red and bright,
But through the scouting she came to find,
nothing could be found that has taken her sight.

She turned to her best friend sharing the search
she could not find,
to the detailed description of a warm nightgown
and color in mind,
to his delight in his mind and heart,
he scouted the stores without her knowing
his mark.

He wanted to seek and find the nightgown she
could wear,
that would someday be hers if he could find it
and share,
that his heart was in line with the love he
had strong,
to bring her the warmth of a red flannel
nightgown that she longed.

All this for her as his love was unfelt,
he wanted her to know just how his heart melts,
so he called to tell her just what he found,
to let her know how he scouted as his excitement
was sound.

She made the call later to find it had taken her
to long,
the disappointment of the red flannel nightgown
gone.
Oh, how she wanted to have the pure warmth,
of the winter day wearing the red nightgown she
had hoped.

She called her best friend to relay,
the message of the nightgown he found for her
did not stay.
He told her, "How sad she had taken to long,"
Her heart just melted thinking, *Oh, well, it
is gone.*

So the eve of Christmas night did come,
she gave him a gift that she hoped he would love.
Then he handed her a gift in a box with a bow,
she opened to find the red flannel nightgown
she had hoped.

 AC LEVENSON

He bought it quickly and swift from the start,
so he could ignite her with a gift that would
steal her heart.
Tears flowed down her cheeks touching the
softness that was spun,
knowing now in her soul her best friend was
the one.

To love and cherish her in a way,
making the commitment that was made to stay,
knowing that the friendship into love did unfold,
into a deep marriage that God surely did mold.

So ought men to love their wives as their
own bodies He that loves his wife loves
himself.

—Ephesians 5:28

THE SACRED JOURNEY

His heart was in the mountain
herding cattle and sheep with a smile.
So simple was he on the love of life,
his heart unsure all the while.

She yearned to be at the little shack
up on the mountain to never look back.
Prayer and the Lord made her cry,
her heart sought the land up high.

Miles and years away, they both prayed.
The Lord showed them the way.
Through the path of our Lord,
both lives broken soon became restored.

Brought together to this place
so strong is this love,
through His amazing grace,
to start a life that that shines from above.

He is like her, she is like him
oh, how this love
came together that glorifies Him.

Their dreams brought them back down,
when their prayers were brought together,
through all of the dark clouds in life,
the desires of their hearts were tethered.

All given to them
as they feel His love,
coming from within His grace from above.

The passion of this love
is not for-bidden,
This is the Lord's plan,
and a gift that was given.

Two hearts joined and have the love of God.
Together in their passion,
whose dreams were proven to be strong.

The un-forbidden journey has only just begun,
their lives will be blessed
and together will become one.

We believe that through the grace, of the
Lord Jesus Christ we shall be saved in
the same manner as they

—Acts 15:11

Together Forever

You and I came through what was very hard.
The arrows came and pain hit our hearts.
We both thought we were coming through,
our lives falling apart not knowing what to do.

Years gone by we came to know,
the hurt and pain we just let go.
Move forward together hand and hand,
letting God take full command.

I look back when we first met,
the passion strong as hard cement,
that had drawn our lives where we should be,
a place we knew as sweet harmony

The sacred ground God holds.
The path of commitment that came to unfold,
the path to hold all that we must.
Love the Lord together "In God We Trust."

Take us home hand and hand,
where you, my Lord, are in command.
This is the time we will show,
the world that marriage can surely glow.

Your hand clasp in mine,
to climb high to His divine.
We both have come to know,
the path of true love brings a glow

Now all glory to God, who is able,
through his mighty power at work
within us, to accomplish infinitely more
than we might ask or think.

—Ephesians 3:20

Unexpected Gift

It came upon a special day when the gift of God did come,
for the ultimate moment, it arose when my heart was won.
I tried so hard to run away to steer away and shift,
to find no way could I escape but come into the unexpected gift.

For my heart did rise and feel the love that I had always dreamed,
I recognized how you cherished that made my soul to gleam.
So through the prayers that helped me know the reason pain had rose,
coming down the path that came to last a love built from God who knows,
the gift was given not understood; our Lord knew the reason to be,
my torn heart and you drifting alone were a path molding us to eternity.
A special day has come for our hearts to trust what was given.

To honor, love, and respect the gift that we know
    came from heaven.

I will cherish you as you cherish me for this gift
is special and true.
We learned that love comes from God so treat it
always like brand new.
How did this happen? to be so good to once
again open up my heart,
I will tell you now that it was unexpected and
was from the very start.

We were not seeking we waited long to
understand the path the Lord had,
to stammer through what came to delight in the
gift at hand.
The unexpected gift, my love, was you coming to
cherish my heart,
and for me to love and lay my heart into your
loving arms

> Love is patient and kind; love does
> not envy or boast; it is not arrogant or
> rude. It does not insist on its own way;
> it is not irritable or resentful; it does
> not rejoice at wrongdoing, but rejoices
> with the truth. Love bears all things,

believes all things, hopes all things,
endures all things. Love never ends.
As for prophecies, they will pass away;
as for tongues, they will cease; as for
knowledge, it will pass away.

—1 Corinthians 13:4–8

WINTER OF TWO THIRTEEN

Her life did start with youth and vigor.
She married, had a son, in hopes of the dream
that delivers.
The promise of goodness and the companions
of life,
that takes our hearts to nothing more than
pure delight.

She learned and churned through hardships
that did come.
She fought the good fight when her heart
was undone.
The time drifted along to another new path,
sinking into the moments hoping it would last.

No reason does surface when the time drifts
on by.
When we thought that our loneliness would not
steal our hearts to die,
into the realm, we try hard not to go,
only to realize the places we ran stopped our
growth.

Growing into places we dreamed would be best,
were the hardest places that our hearts laid
to rest.
Coming back around at the chance once again,
finding love with loneliness was the worst of
the spin.

So she dug into the heart of a little dog,
who brought her into the song that took her out
of the fog.
Holding close to a love she thought could
never be,
into the love of the companion that set her heart
at ease.

We can give up hope to want out of this place.
We wither away feeling only pure disgrace,
wanting no more of what this life can bring,
dreaming again of the pearly gates where our
hearts will sing.

Onward and afraid, she gave up all the hope,
to slide into the place she no more had to cope.
She was lifted into the hands of our Almighty
God,
to see her companion and where loneliness is gone.

Love, peace, and hope are all felt up in heaven.
She was lifted and taken to the security of
our brethren.
Many long years of loneliness and pain are all
gone.
Now at rest and in peace, this she always had
longed.

> For this God is our God forever and
> ever; he will be our guide even unto
> death But God will redeem my soul
> from the power of the grave: for He shall
> receive me.
>
> —Psalms 48:14, 49:15